Love
Your Life

For Sophia and Tobias

⁓

'We find a delight in the beauty and happiness of children,
that makes the heart too big for the body.'

RALPH WALDO EMERSON

Published in 2012 by Hardie Grant Books

Hardie Grant Books (Australia)
Ground Floor, Building 1
658 Church Street
Richmond, Victoria 3121
www.hardiegrant.com.au

Hardie Grant Books (UK)
5th & 6th Floor
52-53 Southwark Street
London SE1 1RU
www.hardiegrant.co.uk

Cataloguing-in-Publication data is available from the
National Library of Australia.

Cover design by Luisa Laino
Text design by Patrick Cannon
Typeset in Adobe Garamond 12/17pt by Cannon Typesetting
Printed and bound in China by 1010

100 ways to start living the life you deserve

Love Your Life

Domonique Bertolucci

Preface

T HE YEAR WAS 1987 and it was a defining
time in my life. I was seventeen and studying for
my university entrance exams. A progressive teacher
at my school had arranged for a motivational speaker
to talk to us about the power of intention, goal setting
and the importance of a positive mindset. Although I
had always been a positive and motivated person, these
ideas had never been explained to me in such simple
and concise terms. It opened my eyes, changed my
world and ultimately led me to the career I have today.

It was not long after this that I was first introduced
to *Illusions* by Richard Bach. I can still recall how
inspired I was, not only by the central theme that we
are each responsible for creating our own reality, but
also by the wonderful idea that any book, regardless
of the topic, could provide us with all the answers we
need—we just have to look for them. What manna to
a book lover.

Over the years, I have collected a library of
motivational, inspirational, spiritual and self-help
books. I've absorbed as much wisdom as I can from

each, but I've also continued to practise the lesson that I first learned when I read *Illusions*; when I'm faced with a challenge and need insight, I close my eyes, focus my mind and allow whatever book I am reading to provide me with the guidance I am looking for.

For the last ten years, I've been writing an extended version of *Love Your Life* as a weekly email to subscribers from all around the world. Rarely a week goes by where I don't receive a message from someone, telling me that this week's message had arrived at exactly the right time and that it was exactly what they needed to read, right now.

This book, *Love Your Life: 100 ways to start living the life you deserve* is a condensed version of those messages. Whether you are looking for inspiration for the day, the right focus for your week or the solution to a problem or challenge, simply close your eyes, open your heart and mind, and allow the book to open. The page before you will contain exactly the inspiration you are seeking … trust me, it works.

Love Your Life, my Monday morning message of inspiration and encouragement, motivation and support, is read by people in more than forty countries.

To subscribe, visit
domoniquebertolucci.com/love-your-life-email

*'If you want to keep your memories,
first you have to live them.'*

BOB DYLAN

Enjoy this moment

While setting goals and planning for the future is important, make sure you give yourself a chance to enjoy your life as it is. Be grateful for each day and take the time to enjoy the life you are living right now.

*'Nothing can add more power to your life
than concentrating all your energies
on a limited set of targets.'*

NIDO QUBEIN

Narrow your focus

Instead of working on a hundred things at once and never completing anything, choose just three tasks to focus on each day. Don't do anything else until these tasks are complete. If you make these tasks your sole focus, not only will you reduce the amount of pressure a giant to-do list places upon you, you will actually get much more done.

'*The true sign of intelligence*
is not knowledge but imagination.'

ALBERT EINSTEIN

Find the time to daydream

The real thing that holds most people back is lack of imagination: they simply can't conceive of the life they want to be living. The only limit to your potential is your imagination, so find some time to daydream about what your life could be like and see what your imagination can come up with.

*'A friend is someone
who understands your past,
believes in your future,
and accepts you just the way you are.'*

ANON.

Be clear who your real friends are

When you decide you want to make changes in your life, your true friends will support you on your path to success and be genuinely happy for you, regardless of their own priorities.

Occasionally you might find that someone you thought was a friend actively tries to undermine your commitment to your goal. If that's the case, it is time to re-evaluate your commitment to them.

*'They can because
they believe they can!'*

Virgil

Be your own cheerleader

Pay attention to your internal dialogue.
Each time you find yourself engaged in self-talk that is negative or limiting in any way,
take a moment to repeat your affirmations—
positive, present-tense, personal statements
about the reality you would like to create.

Keep this up and your subconscious will
soon begin to support, not undermine,
your success.

*'For a tree to become tall
it must grow tough roots among the rocks.'*

FRIEDRICH NIETZSCHE

Never give up

When it feels like life is putting obstacle after obstacle in your path, don't give up. Remind yourself of the goal that you are working towards and how amazing you will feel when you achieve it.

You may need to dust yourself off, adjust your plan or revise your strategy, but whatever you do, don't lose sight of your dream.

*'Failure is often
the line of least persistence.'*

ZIG ZIGLAR

Keep at it

If you find yourself stuck in a rut—unable
to move forward on your goals, yet aware
that by doing nothing you might be moving
backwards—don't panic.

A lack of progress doesn't have to be the
beginning of the end. Just think of one
small, simple step that will help to move
you forward. It doesn't matter if this isn't the
next step in your plan. All that matters is you
keep moving.

*'If error is corrected
whenever it is recognised as such,
the path of error is the path of truth.'*

HANS REICHENBACH

Forget about being perfect

No one gets everything one hundred per cent right, one hundred per cent of the time. What matters is that you gave your best. If something doesn't go according to plan, or you find yourself judging or criticising your performance, remind yourself that you gave your best and your best will always be good enough ... even if you know next time will be even better.

'Destiny is not a matter of chance,
it's a matter of choice.'

JEREMY KITSON

Achieve your potential

Imagine what your life would be like if
you were achieving one hundred per cent
of your potential. If you don't feel you are
already living up to your true potential, don't
panic. Rather than try to change everything
overnight, make a plan to move towards your
destiny a few steps at a time.

Make a commitment to these goals and watch
your destiny become your reality.

'Smile,
breathe
and go slowly.'

THICH NHAT HANH

Do less and achieve more

If you want to get more out of your day, spend time doing less. Find ten minutes each day to recharge your mind and body, and breathe. Taking time out just to breathe will leave you feeling revitalised and energised, with more focus and clarity than ever before.

*'Wealth consists
not in having great possessions,
but in having few wants.'*

EPICTETUS

Be clear about your needs

We actually need very few possessions, so think before you spend. Ask yourself, 'Is this something that I really need, something I simply want or something I will regret buying?' When you can recognise the difference between your wants and needs, your life will become infinitely richer.

'A positive attitude brings strength, energy and initiative.'

REMEZ SASSON

Protect your positive outlook

If you find yourself feeling drained by someone's negative energy, don't try to reason with them, change their mind or convert them to your own positive way. Instead breathe deeply, knowing that your time in their company will pass. Everyone is on their own journey and by conserving your own energy in this way you will ensure that you are not dragged down their path.

'The really efficient labourer will be found not to crowd his day with work, but will saunter to his task surrounded by a wide halo of ease and leisure.'

HENRY DAVID THOREAU

Make your life easier

There will always be more you *could* be doing, but that doesn't mean they are things you *should* be doing. Instead of trying to race through your to-do list, crossing off every item as fast as you can, leave your old paradigm behind and ask yourself, 'How can I make my life easier?' Use your answer to remove as many things as you can from your list completely.

'Life is a rollercoaster,
you've just gotta ride it.'

RONAN KEATING

Enjoy the ride

If you feel like life is an uphill battle, remind yourself that you don't have to climb the hill. It's something that you are choosing to do because you know that the reward will be worth it in the long term.

When you find yourself feeling overwhelmed by obstacles, if the right move for you is to walk away, then do it. If deep in your heart you know you need to carry on, take a big breath and hold on for the ride.

'Mediocrity is self-inflicted.
Genius is self-bestowed.'

Walter Russell

Be the best you can be

Focus on being the best you can be, in all that you do. You might not be flawless and you may still encounter ups and downs, but you will be able to relax, confident in the knowledge that it couldn't have been any better than it was.

*'I don't know the key to success,
but the key to failure
is trying to please everybody.'*

BILL COSBY

You can't keep everyone happy

If you find yourself feeling that no matter what you do, someone will be disappointed, stop and take a minute to reconnect with what it is that you want and what will make you happy.

While it's not realistic to suggest that you will always be able to put your own wants first, unless you know what they are, they will never stand a chance.

*'Feel the fear
and do it anyway.'*

SUSAN JEFFERS

Step outside your comfort zone

A great way to boost your confidence and self-belief is to step outside of your comfort zone and do something that scares you.

If there is something you would like to do but have lacked the courage to attempt, challenge yourself to be brave.

Now is your moment.

*'If we are facing in the right direction,
all we have to do is keep on walking.'*

BUDDHIST PROVERB

Be consistent

Make a commitment to being consistent.
While it's easy to stay focused when
everything is going your way, it's much
tougher to stay on track on the days that just
feel like hard work. Regardless of the kind
of day you are having, stay focused on your
goals and keep up the good work.

'Dreams do come true,
if only we wish hard enough.'

JAMES BARRIE

Give yourself permission to dream

If you want to live your best life, don't make the mistake of dismissing your dreams as soon as they pop into your head. Take the time to explore them. This doesn't mean that every single thought needs to be acted upon, just that your ideas shouldn't be dismissed without thought or consideration.

'Do what you can,
with what you have,
where you are.'

THEODORE ROOSEVELT

Celebrate your personal best

Everyone is different; we all learn different things at different times and what is easy for one person might be an enormous challenge for another. Being the best you can be is about setting your own goals and recognising when you have achieved them, rather than trying to boost your self-esteem through the praise or recognition of others. Celebrate your personal best and leave everyone else to focus on theirs.

*'Without deviation,
progress is not possible.'*

FRANK ZAPPA

Express your gratitude

Don't chastise, criticise or judge yourself for
the things you haven't done. Life is a journey,
not a destination. As long as your intention
is to live your best possible life, this is the life
you will be living.

Forget about all the things you haven't done
and instead express your gratitude for all
the experiences your life has been filled with
so far.

*'If you ask what is the single
most important key to longevity,
I would have to say
it is avoiding worry, stress and tension.'*

GEORGE F. BURNS

Learn to let it go

Raise your awareness to the source of stress in your life and the level of influence or control you have over each stressor. If you can't do anything about it, breathe and let it go. Taking a moment to refocus in this way gives you a sense of empowerment and has an immediate, positive impact on your stress levels.

'Change the changeable,
accept the unchangeable
and remove yourself from the unacceptable.'

DENIS WAITLEY

Reinvent yourself

It's easy to find excuses for not living up to your potential; it's much harder to do something about it. If you find yourself complaining about the same aspect of your life over and over … stop!

Take a deep breath and put the energy you usually spend on complaining towards reinventing that part of your life.

'Everything that irritates us about others can lead us to an understanding of ourselves.'

CARL JUNG

Focus on what you are getting right

When you are criticising other people and their failings, deep down all you are doing is trying to make yourself feel better about your own. Rather than focusing on what everyone else is getting wrong, give your confidence an authentic boost by focusing on all you are getting right.

*'You should always be aware
that your head creates your world.'*

KEN KEYES JR

Listen to your inner dialogue

Any time you find yourself engaging in negative self-talk, reform your thoughts with a positive affirmation, reframe your thoughts with logic or simply ignore them altogether.

While you might not be able to stop the little voice in your head, you can choose which conversations you will participate in and which ones you need to ignore.

'The idealists and visionaries, foolish enough to throw caution to the winds ... have advanced mankind and have enriched the world.'

EMMA GOLDMAN

Stay true to your dreams

If you find that other people are not able
to share in your vision or believe in your
goals, don't let them prick your balloon.
Instead, realise their response is based on
the expectations they have for their own
lives and that this doesn't have to affect the
expectations you have for yours.

'Often the difference between a successful man
and a failure
is not one's better abilities or ideas,
but the courage that one has to bet on his ideas,
to take a calculated risk—and to act.'

MAXWELL MALTZ

Don't let fear get in your way

One of the biggest mistakes people make is to allow fear to get in the way of their success. Just because you are experiencing fear doesn't mean that you can't do something—it just means that doing it is going to feel uncomfortable. Learn to get comfortable with discomfort and carry on regardless.

'*There is only one success:*
to be able to spend your life your own way.'

CHRISTOPHER MORLEY

Do what you want to do

It's so easy to spend your time doing things you feel obligated to do, never allowing time for the things that you really want to do. At the start of each day, think about how you would like your day to play out: what you would like to achieve, where you would like to expend your energy and, importantly, what you would like *not* to do.

Then choose one thing that you are *not* going to do and commit to *not* doing it!

*'I will study and get ready
and someday my chance will come.'*

ABRAHAM LINCOLN

Believe in yourself

Commit to believing in yourself, unconditionally. Any time you find yourself engaged in negative or limiting self-talk, stop. It might take a little practice at first, but if you refuse to entertain thoughts that don't serve your ambitions, you will quickly make room for all those that do.

'Don't sweat the small stuff …
and it's all small stuff.'

RICHARD CARLSON

Let your values guide you

Next time you find yourself faced with analysis paralysis, stop. Forget the pros and cons and instead ask yourself, 'Which of my options will take me closer to a life that is in alignment with my values?'

Once you know the answer to this question, knowing which option to take will be obvious.

'Abundance is not something we acquire.
It is something we tune into.'

WAYNE DYER

Count your blessings

It's easy to spend so much energy striving for
the things you want that you lose sight of
all that you have. If you want to experience
true wealth and abundance in your life, look
around you and make a point of appreciating
what you already have.

*'Let there be more joy
and laughter in your living.'*

EILEEN CADDY

Focus on your time off

If you want true balance in your life, managing the way you spend your time 'off' must become just as important as the way you manage your time 'on'. Look at the hours that you don't spend at work and make a plan to use your time in the most refreshing, revitalising and rewarding way possible.

*'The shortest way to do many things
is to do only one thing at once.'*

SAMUEL SMILES

Don't multi-task

The only real way to get lots of things done
is to focus on doing only one thing at a time;
the power of multi-tasking is a myth. Ten
per cent of ten things isn't a hundred per cent
of anything.

Give each task that you are working on one
hundred per cent of your attention and you
will be amazed at how much you get done.

*'The best thing to hold onto in life
is each other.'*

AUDREY HEPBURN

Give the people you love the best of you

Don't allow the people that matter most in your life to be pushed to the bottom of your to-do list. Make your loved ones your priority; give them your time and your energy and give it to them before you exhaust yourself taking care of all the other stuff that fills up your life.

'*They cannot take away our self-respect*
if we do not give it to them.'

MAHATMA GANDHI

Don't take offence

When someone does or says something that bothers you, rather than getting all riled up, preserve your energy and learn to let things slide. That doesn't mean that what the other person has said or done is 'okay'. Just remind yourself that you get to choose the thoughts and actions that have an impact on your life and you can choose to not allow the negative ones to bother you.

'If you know you want it,
have it.'

GITA BELLIN

Never apologise for your dreams

If you find yourself apologising for what you want out of life, stop. It is your life and you deserve to fill it with the things that matter most to you. You don't need anyone else's approval to live your best life, so don't waste energy looking for it.

*'Excuses are the nails
used to build a house of failure.'*

DON WILDER

Don't make excuses

If you are not already living your best life, the one thing that really needs to change is you. Of course life might be even better if some of the circumstances around you changed too, but unless you take responsibility for the way you live, your best life will always be a long way off.

'*When you have to make a choice
and don't make it,
that is in itself a choice.*'

WILLIAM JAMES

Own your choices

Life is full of choices. Of course with the wisdom of hindsight you may wish you had chosen a different option, but until you find that crystal ball, the best you can do is to make mindful choices based on the information that is available now.

The only wrong decision is indecision. Every time you make a conscious choice, you are making the right choice for you, right now.

'It's never too late
to be who you might have been.'

GEORGE ELIOT

Now is the time

If you catch yourself thinking that it's too late to change your life, you're wrong. The passing of time is never a valid excuse for not going after the things you want in life.

You deserve to do, be and have all that you want from life and there will never be a better moment than right now to start making it happen.

*'You can only grow
if you are willing to feel
awkward and uncomfortable
when you try something new.'*

BRIAN TRACY

Change your life

When you're busy, it's easy to fall into a rut where you do the same thing over and over, partly because it's easy, but also because you can't find the energy or inspiration to do things differently.

Step outside your comfort zone and change your daily routine. There's nothing like a change of scene to remind you that the world is full of possibilities; it's simply up to you to choose which ones to seize.

*'Things turn out best
for the people who make the best
out of the way things turn out.'*

ART LINKLETTER

Focus on what you have

Each day, before you start focusing on your goals, wants, wishes and desires, take a moment to think of one thing that you are truly grateful for in your life. By focusing on what you already have, you will find it much easier to pursue the things you truly want.

'Happiness is that state of consciousness
which proceeds from
the achievement of one's values.'

AYN RAND

Be clear about what really matters

If you feel you are being pulled in many different directions, making the right decisions can seem hard. The key is to check in with your values. When you are clear on what matters most to you, deciding where and how to focus your energies will be easy.

'To achieve the impossible dream,
try going to sleep.'

Anon.

Get a good night's sleep

Lack of, or poor quality, sleep will have a big impact on your ability to stay positive, motivated and focused on your goals.

Commit to making a good night's sleep a priority in your life. Go to bed at a sensible time and spend the last five or ten minutes of each day reflecting, first on all the things you were grateful for that day, and then on your intentions for the next.

*'Judge a person by their questions,
rather than their answers.'*

VOLTAIRE

Don't judge others

As adults we are all free to live our lives in accordance with our own principles, but so often people judge each other for what is ultimately a difference in values. Rather than criticising others for having differing values, focus your energy on honouring yours.

'There is but one cause of human failure
and that is man's lack of faith in his true Self.'

WILLIAM JAMES

Give your confidence a boost

Often people are so busy concentrating on what they need to improve about themselves, they forget to consider all the things they are already getting right. Make a list of all of your good qualities, the things that you are proud of and the successes you have had in life and give your confidence a boost by focusing on what's great about you.

'The only difference between
"marital" and "martial"
is where you put the "I".'

MITCH ALBOM

Put yourself in their shoes

Conflict is a natural part of life, but as an argument heats up it is easy to lose sight of the other person's perspective. And the more we hold onto our ego, the 'I' in the conflict, the more fuel we throw on the fire.

When this happens, challenge yourself to see the other person's point of view. Once you genuinely engage with how they are feeling, you will find it much easier to disengage your ego and find a solution that works for everyone.

*'A good life is not lived by chance
but by choice.'*

KOBI YAMADA

Make conscious choices

It is easy to fall into the trap of looking at other people and assuming that they are living a happier or more fulfilling life because they are luckier than you. They're not.

The real reason some people find happiness and meaning in their lives while others don't is all about the choices they make. Choose to live a fulfilling life and ensure every other decision you make supports this intention.

*'Winning starts
with beginning!'*

ROBERT SCHULLER

Take one step at a time

If you have a goal you have been thinking about for a while but have had a tough time making progress, ask yourself, 'Is this something I really want to achieve?'

If you discover that it's not really important to you, let it go … cross it off your list forever. If it is genuinely important to you, commit to moving forward at least one step. You don't have to achieve your goal in its entirety, but don't let anything get in the way of making a start!

'Some men see things
as they are and say "why?"
I dream things that never were
and say "why not?"'

R. F. KENNEDY

Look for inspiration

If you are looking for inspiration, ask yourself, 'Am I the first person to ever want this for my life? Am I the first person to ever have this dream?'

In the vast majority of cases the answer will be no. There will be many other people who have achieved, or are achieving, the very same things you want for your life. Seek out people who inspire you and learn as much as you can from them.

*'Man cannot discover new oceans
until he has courage to lose sight of the shore.'*

ANDRÉ GIDE

Release yourself

Imagine a future where there are no limits
on who you can become and what you can
achieve. Each time you find yourself saying
'but' to the ideas you have for your vision,
release yourself from your preconceived limits
and give yourself permission to achieve your
true potential.

'Gratitude helps you to grow and expand;
gratitude brings joy and laughter into your life
and into the lives of all those around you.'

EILEEN CADDY

Recognise how fortunate you really are

Take a minute to think about how fortunate you are. While your life may not be perfect and there may still be things you would like to do, be or have, chances are there is a lot of good in your life.

Before you begin to think about your goals and what you would like to achieve, make sure you recognise the abundance in your life right now.

'Enjoy the little things,
for one day you may look back
and realise they were the big things.'

ROBERT BRAULT

Enjoy the life you already have

Achieving your goals for the future is important, but don't let these desires overtake your life. Enjoying the here and now is just as vital.

If you find yourself racing through your day, not thinking about anything other than the next thing you have to get done, stop. Look around you and find one thing to take simple pleasure in. You will find yourself enjoying the life you already have so much more.

'*Right now a moment of time is passing by …
we must become that moment.*'

PAUL CÉZANNE

Learn to be present

Whether you are at work, play or somewhere in between, make an effort to simply focus on what you are doing right now. Learn to be present in each and every moment of your life and with the people with whom you share it.

Don't think about coulds or shoulds, what-ifs or maybes. Just keep your mind on the here and now and appreciate the moment for what it is.

'*The quality of your attention
determines the quality of other people's thinking.*'

NANCY KLINE

Listen well

This week, whenever you are in conversation with someone, give them one hundred per cent of your attention. Don't interrupt and don't think of how you might respond until after they have finished speaking.

It's amazing the difference the quality of your listening will make to the conversations you are having.

*'Your goals, minus your doubts,
equal your reality.'*

RALPH MARSTON

Get out of the way

If you find yourself holding back from taking the next steps towards your goal, ask yourself 'What is really getting in my way here?'

More often than not, the answer will be you: your belief in yourself, your belief in your ability to achieve your goal … or both. When you find yourself with a list of things that you need to achieve before you can make real progress on your goal, take a leap of faith and go for it regardless.

*'Nothing ever becomes real
till it is experienced.'*

JOHN KEATS

Take a moment to dream.

When life gets hectic, it can be hard to
remember what your dreams are, let alone see
them as a potential reality. The best remedy
is to make time to visualise your dreams as if
they were your reality. If you can spend five
minutes each day visualising your dreams, not
only will they start to feel possible, they will
start to *become* possible.

*'Until you try,
you don't know what you can't do.'*

Henry James

Live boldly

If you have an audacious goal, the very thought of it can overwhelm you to the point of inertia. Often this lack of activity is the result of fear. Fear of failing in your attempts to achieve your goal and fear of how your life will change if you do.

When you find yourself feeling afraid, the most important thing is to simply do something. Don't worry if it seems like baby steps; what matters is that you don't let fear impede your progress.

'Sometimes there is no easy way out,
but there is always an easier way out
and a harder way out.
Choose wisely.'

NATHANIEL BRONNER JR

Look for an easier way

This week, if you find yourself hitting a stumbling block, instead of trying to use all of your will and determination to force your way through, stop and ask yourself, 'Is there an easier way?' While the path of least resistance is rarely the right one, the path of less resistance might be just the shortcut to success you need.

*'Let nothing dim the light
that shines from within.'*

MAYA ANGELOU

Don't let others bring you down

When someone is negative, judgemental or critical towards you, don't fall into the trap of blaming them for making you feel bad. Remind yourself that nobody can make you feel anything. It's entirely up to you how you choose to feel. What they are doing is providing you with the opportunity to feel bad and inviting you to join them in putting you down. It's up to you to accept or reject the invitation.

'There is no such thing as a problem without a gift for you in its hands.'

RICHARD BACH

Accept the challenge

When you find yourself facing a challenging situation, don't succumb to endlessly exploring the cause of the problem or seeking to attribute blame. Instead, ask yourself what you can learn from this situation and how this experience will help you grow.

'The most important thing is to
enjoy your life—to be happy—
it's all that matters.'

AUDREY HEPBURN

Choose to be happy

Being happy doesn't have to be complicated. The minute you make the decision to be happy, you instantly become happier. Your perspective shifts and you start to see your world from the vantage point of someone who is happy. Choosing to be happy isn't the only thing that you need to do, but unless you make the conscious decision to be happy, your other efforts will be wasted.

'Thoughts ... crystallise into habit and habit solidifies into circumstances.'

JAMES ALLEN

Take one step closer

Most goals are a long way off until you make some progress towards them. If the thought of getting started on your goal feels overwhelming, the key is to take small steps, but to take them consistently.

Make the commitment to doing one small thing each day that takes you closer to your dreams.

'Be careful the environment you choose
for it will shape you;
be careful the friends you choose
for you will become like them.'

W. CLEMENT STONE

Choose your friends wisely

When you think about your friends and the people you spend your time with, examine whether they hold compatible values, share similar ideals and support you in your dreams, goals and ambitions.

Make sure that the people you call your friends are people who really belong in your life.

'*Our doubts are traitors,*
and make us lose the good
we might oft win by fearing to attempt.'

WILLIAM SHAKESPEARE

Back yourself

If there is something you want to achieve in life, the first and most important step is to decide to back yourself. Make the decision to believe in your dreams unconditionally and then do whatever it takes to make those dreams your reality.

*'Reality is something
you rise above.'*

LIZA MINNELLI

Choose the best way forward

Not everything in life will go your way. Some things will be easy, some things harder and sometimes it can feel like everything and everyone is against you. What makes all the difference is how you navigate the unexpected twists and turns that life inevitably takes.

When things don't go your way, don't let it bring you down. Instead, take a deep breath, look at your options and simply choose the best way forward for now.

'Do or do not.
There is no try.'

YODA

Create helpful habits

If you find yourself trying to change certain behaviours, only to quickly give up and go back to your old ways because it feels too hard, don't criticise yourself for not trying hard enough. Instead, focus on creating a new habit, one that in a very short period of time will feel natural, automatic and, best of all, be easy to stick to.

'The main thing is keeping the main thing the main thing.'

STEPHEN COVEY

Do the things that matter

When the pace of your life means that you are constantly rushing from pillar to post, you can find yourself resenting things you could be enjoying. Before you exhaust yourself trying to do everything, ask yourself, 'What really matters?' Focus on doing this and letting go of the rest.

*'There is more to us than we know.
If we can be made to see it,
perhaps for the rest of our lives
we will be unwilling to settle for less.'*

KURT HAHN

Don't limit your potential

When you were young you believed that anything was possible. Like most people, as you grew older, you were probably told that you needed to be realistic about what you wanted from life. Don't limit your potential. Challenge the notion of what is realistic in life and simply focus on what you want.

'Nothing is impossible.
The word itself says "I'm possible"!'

AUDREY HEPBURN

Your daydreams hold the answer

Too often people think that their daydreams are an indulgence, when in fact they can be a powerful insight into the life you really want to be living.

At the end of each daydreaming session, make a note of the ideas or themes that have been amusing your mind. This will give you great insight into some of the essential elements of your best life.

*'It is not the man who has too little,
but the man who craves more, that is poor.'*

SENECA

Choose abundance

The experience of wealth and abundance is a state of mind. The easiest way to achieve this state is not to focus on all the things you wish you had, but to think of all the things you do have. You will never feel poor if you can recognise how rich your life is already.

*'To be what we are,
and to become
what we are capable of becoming
is the only end of life.'*

R. L. STEVENSON

Honour your values

Do you sometimes find that as hard as you work at being happier, you only seem to feel more conflicted? If you find yourself with a decision to make or an option to consider, ask yourself, 'Does this take me closer to, or further from, a life that is aligned with my values?'

True happiness is achieved when we live our life in alignment with our values and honour the things that matter most in our life.

'It is a commonplace observation
that work expands so as to
fill the time available for its completion.'

C. NORTHCOTE PARKINSON

Learn to prioritise

Most people act as if every single item on their to-do list is of equal importance. In reality, this is rarely the case. To-do lists usually contain things that are urgent, things that are really important and a whole lot of other *stuff*. All too often, it's the stuff that gets the most attention.

If you focus on the most important things first, you'll get so much more out of your day.

'I live for those who love me,
for those who know me true.'

GEORGE LINNAEUS BANKS

Be mindful of the company you keep

Surround yourself with people who are supportive of your ambitions and who encourage you to be the best you can be. Make the decision to spend most of your time with people who are as passionate as you are about the plans you have for your life.

*'If you refuse to accept anything but the best,
you very often get it!'*

W. Somerset Maugham

Don't settle for less than what you deserve

It takes courage to live your best life.
While it is important to be willing to make
conscious compromises in life, hidden
compromises are those that you don't realise
you are making.

Be brave and make sure that the vision
you have is for the best possible life you
can imagine.

*'Though no one can go back
and make a brand-new start,
anyone can start from now
and make a brand-new ending.'*

CARL BARD

Get back to basics

If you feel like you need to reinvent yourself in order to achieve your potential, rather than exhaust yourself by making a list of a million changes, get back to basics.

The key to achieving any goal, big or small, is to start with small achievable changes. Decide what yours will be and start the journey to your best life today.

'Good ideas are not adopted automatically. They must be driven into practice with courageous impatience.'

HYMAN RICKOVER

Get in the driver's seat

Instead of thinking of reasons why your dreams can't become reality, focus on all the reasons why they can.

When you think of your goals, think of why you deserve to have them in your life and exactly what you are going to do to get them.

'Don't ask yourself what the world needs.
Ask yourself what makes you come alive,
and then go do that.
Because what the world needs is
people who have come alive.'

HAROLD THURMAN

Do the things you love

There is a big difference between doing what you're good at and doing what you love. The sweet spot is when you get to do both.

Ask yourself, 'What do I love doing?' and then make sure you find some time to do this. It doesn't have to be all day, everyday—even spending just one hour doing something you are passionate about will refresh, energise and invigorate your life.

'Things do not change;
we change!'

HENRY DAVID THOREAU

Put it into action

At the end of each day, take a minute to reflect on how your day turned out and then think of one thing you could do differently tomorrow.

You can learn so much by reflecting, non-judgementally, on your experiences. Don't ask yourself, 'What did I get wrong?' Simply look back over the day and ask yourself, 'What could I do differently?' Then commit to putting this change into action.

*'The difference between what we do,
and what we are capable of doing,
would suffice to solve most of the
world's problems.'*

MAHATMA GANDHI

You can achieve anything you want

When you find yourself thinking about things you could do if only time or money or circumstances were different, what is really stopping you are limiting beliefs in who you are and what you can achieve.

While your circumstances may be less than ideal, stories abound of people who have achieved amazing things with little or no resources. See yourself as one of those people and start to believe that you can achieve anything you want, if you are willing to go for it.

'Not he who has much is rich,
but he who gives much.'

ERICH FROMM

Recognise how much you have to give

Generosity is not just about money. To be truly generous, you need to give your time, energy and spirit as well. What you give in life will determine what you receive, so give of yourself in abundance.

'If you want to be happy, be.'

LEO TOLSTOY

Don't wait for happiness

So many people are *waiting* to feel happy.
They think they will be happy when they've
done this or achieved that. But the truth
is, enduring happiness is not a result of the
things you've done, but the person you've
chosen to be.

*'Your life will be defined
as much by the things you say no to,
as the things to which you say yes.'*

ANON.

Learn to say no

Making a compromise isn't a bad thing; a rich and interesting life will always be filled with options, and compromises are an essential part of getting what you want out of life.

When faced with a decision, ask yourself, 'Will taking this path feel like a compromise, or will it leave me feeling compromised?' Once you know the answer, you can say yes or no to the option presented, safe in the knowledge that you are still pursuing your best life.

*'Lust is easy. Love is hard.
Like is most important.'*

CARL REINER

Show your love

Throughout your life, different people will come to mean different things to you. There are crushes you thought you'd never get over, but did. Friendships you thought would last forever, yet didn't. Through it all, most people are lucky enough to have a few special friends whom they will always hold dear.

When you find yourself thinking of someone special in your life, rather than just assuming they know, make a point of telling or showing them exactly how much they mean to you.

*'People begin to become successful
the minute they decide to be!'*

HARVEY MACKAY

Set yourself up for success

When you set yourself unrealistic goals, all you are really doing is setting yourself up for failure. If you want to be successful, you need to set yourself up for success. Take a good hard look at your goals, actions or to-do lists and make sure that you genuinely believe they can be achieved.

Don't try to achieve the impossible and fail. Instead, achieve the achievable and succeed.

'There are no real successes without rejection.
The more rejection you get, the better you are,
the more you've learned,
the closer you are to your outcome.'

ANTHONY ROBBINS

Boost your staying power

So often there is a timing difference between effort and reward, between the work you are doing and the results you are seeking. Don't see these delays as failures; don't let the disappointments and frustrations get you down.

Remember, what matters isn't how quickly you succeed, but that you don't give up until you succeed.

*'Nothing would be done at all
if a man waited until he could do it so well
that noone could find fault with it.'*

CARDINAL NEWMAN

Let go of your excuses

Any time you find yourself making a direct
or indirect excuse for something in your
life, realise that what you are really doing is
accepting a limiting belief.

Learn to let go of your excuses and discover
what life can be like when the only limits you
accept are ones you consciously choose.

'Ideas by themselves
cannot produce a change of being;
your efforts must go in the right direction,
and one must correspond with the other.'

P. D. OUSPENSKY

Expend your energy wisely

One of the great benefits of being clear on your values is being able to discern what things deserve your time and energy and what things are simply not worth the bother.

If you find yourself stressed, tense or anxious about something, ask yourself, 'Does this really matter to me?' When you know the answer, you will easily be able to determine if the situation warrants your time and energy, or if the best course of action is to simply let it slide.

*'We don't have an eternity
to realise our dreams,
only the time we are here.'*

SUSAN TAYLOR

Do the first things first

If you find you are so busy getting stuff done that you never get around to making progress on the things that really matter, put first things first.

Before you worry about all the miscellany on your to do list, focus on doing one thing each day that takes you closer to the life of your dreams.

'Courage is not the absence of fear,
but rather the judgement
that something else
is more important than fear.'

AMBROSE REDMOON

Be fearless in your decisions

When you find yourself tossing and turning between two different options, unable to move forward and make a decision, the real cause of this inert state is often not lack of clarity but lack of courage. Courage to accept that there is no perfect decision and whichever one you make will have consequences, both positive and negative.

If you find yourself in this state, don't waste energy endlessly weighing up the pros and cons. Instead, be fearless in your decision and move forward with confidence.

*'There is no scarcity of opportunity
to make a living at what you love;
there's only scarcity of resolve to make it happen.'*

WAYNE DYER

Make a commitment

While there may be many things you need to do or achieve to make a dream for your future a reality, the only thing that really matters is that you commit fully to making it a reality in your life. No other thought or action will ever be as important as this one.

'Most people would rather be
certain they're miserable
than risk being happy.'

ROBERT ANTHONY

Don't be complacent

It won't always be easy to do, be or have everything you want in life, but if your desires are genuine, over time these things will begin to come to you with ease. On those occasions when striving for your goals does feel like hard work and your motivation is not as strong as it could be, remind yourself that an ordinary life will always be the easier option. It's just not the right option for you.

*'He who has begun his task
has half done it.'*

HORACE

Begin it now

The fastest way to get something done is to get it done. When there are things you need to do that feel difficult or challenging, don't give into the urge to put them off. Instead, make a start and relax, confident in the knowledge that you are already halfway there.

*'The bond that links your true family
is not one of blood,
but of respect and joy in each other's life.'*

RICHARD BACH

Cherish your family

Families are a complicated mix of people who, despite loving you dearly, may not always be able to share in your hopes and dreams for the future. Your true friends, however, are people you are drawn to precisely because of shared values, goals, ideals and beliefs. Let these people form part of your family and treasure them the same way as you would if they were your flesh and blood.

'Success is the ability to go from one failure to another with no loss of enthusiasm.'

Winston Churchill

Keep the faith

Failure and setbacks are a part of life, but when they are happening to you it can be hard not to lose faith in your goal or, worse, faith in yourself.

If something doesn't go your way, don't lose enthusiasm. Keep focused on your goal and know that even if the success you desire is currently out of sight, it really is just around the corner.

'When I was young I observed
that nine out of ten things I did were failures.
I didn't want to be a failure,
so I did ten times more work.'

GEORGE BERNARD SHAW

Do what needs to be done

If the things you really want in life seem out of reach, don't give up. You can achieve anything you want, but you have to be willing to work for it. When hurdles get in your way, meet your obstacles head on and do whatever you need to do to move forward.

*'The absence of alternatives
clears the mind marvellously.'*

HENRY KISSINGER

Make a bold gesture

Sometimes the easiest way to commit to your goal is to make a public declaration, bold gesture or other commitment that makes getting out of it much harder. In an ideal world you would never need external pressures to help you stick to your goal, but occasionally a little outside pressure is exactly the encouragement you need.

*'Focus your attention
on your intention.'*

ANON.

Focus on the outcome

It serves no purpose to expend your energy thinking about the things you haven't done and the goals you haven't achieved. Focus your thoughts on the outcomes you do want and watch them become your reality.

*'If you have built castles in the air
your work need not be lost;
that is where they should be.
Now put the foundations under them.'*

HENRY DAVID THOREAU

Build a solid foundation

If you set out to achieve a goal and it doesn't go your way, don't fall into the trap of feeling that you have wasted your time or that you should give up. Use your setbacks as an opportunity to review your plans and work out what you need to do differently next time to give yourself the best chance of success.

*'No one can get inner peace
by pouncing on it!'*

HARRY EMERSON FOSDICK

Be balanced about balance

It really isn't possible to achieve a perfectly balanced day, every day of your life. Rather than criticising yourself because one aspect of your life was out of balance today, simply make sure that the needs you have in that part of your life are met tomorrow.

'Life is not measured
by the number of breaths we take
but by the moments that take our breath away.'

HILARY COOPER

The choice is yours

Ultimately, how you live your life is up to you. You can pursue material possessions, external validation and the satisfaction of your ego, or you can choose to make genuine happiness your goal: a life where you cherish your loved ones, honour your values and focus on being the best you can be.

Acknowledgements

MY FIRST THANKS as always go to my wonderful agent Tara Wynne at Curtis Brown for her never-ending belief in my work, and to all the team at Hardie Grant for once again being such a pleasure to work with.

To all my clients, past and present, and the inspiring people who attend my workshops and courses, thank you for inviting me to be a part of your journey. It is an honour and a privilege and my life is infinitely richer for the experience.

Thank you to all the people I consider my family, both related and chosen, including my mum and dad, Jeff, Laurel, Alecia, Tristan, Brooke, Tamy, Kate, Mary, Lisa and Polly. I wouldn't be who I am, or where I am, without your love and endless support.

To my precious Toby, thank you for proving that good things come to those who wait. To my darling Sophia, for providing me with endless joy. And to Paul, for everything, always.

About the Author

DOMONIQUE BERTOLUCCI is the author of *The Happiness Code: Ten keys to being the best you can be*, and the closely guarded secret behind some of the country's most successful people.

Passionate about living your life on your own terms, Domonique has a client list that reads like a who's who of CEOs and corporate figures, award-winning entrepreneurs and celebrities, and her workshops are attended by people from all walks of life, from all around the world.

Since writing her first book, *Your Best Life*, in 2006, Domonique has become Australia's most popular life coach. More than ten million people have seen, read or heard her advice.

Domonique divides her time between Sydney and London. She lives with her husband and young family and in her spare time can be found with her nose in a book, watching a movie, or keeping up the great Italian tradition of feeding the people that you love.

domoniquebertolucci.com
facebook.com/domoniquebertolucci
twitter.com/fromDomonique